Gillen

This booklet was written by Jonathan Yates, Research Analyst at GillenMarkets, and is also available in eBook format (PDF, Epub or Kindle).

About Gillen

Gillen is a boutique investment advisor offering expert advice on the management of personal, pension and corporate monies. We place a strong emphasis on fully understanding our clients' needs, so that we can make informed decisions and plans, together.

We are investment advisors, not product sellers. Our investment solutions are structured to meet the specific needs of each individual client with minimum assets of €500k.

Our investment advisory fee structure aligns our interests with yours, ensuring that we sit on the same side of the table as our clients.

With our fee structure, there are:

- No upfront commissions or fees payable by clients.

- No dealing costs.

- No early redemption penalties.

- No VAT.

Just a transparent 1.0% annual advisory fee on the assets under advice.

We also offer a subscription-based investment newsletter for do-it-yourself investors and training courses both in-person and online for those wishing to learn more about the principles of sound investing.

We believe trust is earned. Our belief is that we work for clients, looking at each individual's needs and taking a commonsense, long-term approach.

We have built an outstanding team with the depth of knowledge and experience to meet all our clients' investment needs. We have an appetite for learning and sharing and we always partner with our clients as equals.

We'd like to hear from you!

Contact details

T: + 353 (0)1 287 1400
E: info@gillenmarkets.com
W: www.gillenmarkets.com

Follow us on Facebook, LinkedIn, Twitter and Gillenmarkets.com.

ILTB Ltd (trading as Gillen/GillenMarkets) is regulated by the Central Bank of Ireland.

Private Equity: Access for All

Investing in Private Equity through the Stock Markets

A **GillenMarkets** Publication

Jonathan Yates

Published by OAK TREE PRESS, Cork T12 XY2N
www.oaktreepress.com / www.SuccessStore.com

© 2023 ILTB Ltd t/a GillenMarkets

A catalogue record of this book is available from the British Library.

ISBN 978 1 78119 565 9 (Paperback)
ISBN 978 1 78119 566 6 (PDF)
ISBN 978 1 78119 567 3 (ePub)
ISBN 978 1 78119 568 0 (Kindle)

Disclaimer
Investing carries risk and none of the stocks or funds highlighted in this booklet constitute a recommendation by the author, GillenMarkets or the publisher and none of these parties can assume liability for any losses that may be sustained should a reader subsequently invest in them, and any such liability is hereby disclaimed. Readers should take professional advice before making any investment. None of the material in this publication constitutes investment advice or an offer to invest in any of the funds referred to. No one receiving this publication should treat it as a personal recommendation as it does not take into account the needs and objectives, personal circumstances, including investment experience, financial position, or attitude to risk of recipients.
Warning
Past performance is not a reliable guide to future performance.

CONTENTS

Gillen.

Other Publications from GillenMarkets

3 STEPS TO INVESTMENT SUCCESS (2012)
How to Obtain the Returns While Controlling the Risk

Rory Gillen

A PATH TO FINANCIAL FREEDOM (2nd edition / 2023)
A Guide to Sound Investing

Rory Gillen

TIMING THE MARKETS (2023)
Unemotional Approaches to Making Buy & Sell Decisions in Markets

Rory Gillen

BRICKS & MORTAR THROUGH STOCKS & SHARES (2023)
Property Investing in the Stock Markets

Darren Gillen

INTELLIGENT GOLD INVESTING (2nd edition / 2023)
Including a Section on Bitcoin

Rory Gillen

UNDERSTANDING ALTERNATIVE ASSETS (2nd edition / 2023)
Gold, Forestry, Government & Corporate Bonds, Renewable Energy &
Hedge Strategies

Rory Gillen

All available in print and ebook formats from
GillenMarkets.com, SuccessStore.com & Amazon

The prospect of above average returns has always made private equity an attractive sub-sector of investing in financial markets. Simply put, private equity refers to investments in non-publicly listed companies, either through ownership of the company or an interest in the entity – with specialised, long-term focused managers taking stakes in private companies with the aim of growing these companies over time.

In Ireland, the principal way for investors to gain exposure has been through third-party international private equity funds made available or distributed by Irish-based stockbrokers, which often come with substantial initial investment requirements and long-term lock-in periods (making them illiquid investments).

For retail investors, these high minimum investment levels and the prospect of having to lock away money for many years can take a considerable amount of the shine off such private equity offerings. In addition, the fact that stockbrokers and other product sellers offering up these investments are getting paid based on the amount of money raised for a fund offering creates an inevitable conflict of interest.

All is not lost, however, as, in our view, the UK listed private equity sector, a universe of listed private equity funds, offers what we consider to be a far better alternative. Even a small investor can invest in private equity *via* high-quality, liquid funds listed on the London Stock Exchange without the burden of high minimum investment levels, long-term lock-in periods or onerous upfront fees, but which have also historically delivered the attractive returns we have seen from their unlisted private equity counterparts.

With that in mind, this booklet aims to inform the reader about the key considerations in private equity investing. We first take you through the background of private equity markets – from the first boom of leveraged buyouts in the 1980s to today's market which is valued at around $6.3 trillion globally.

We then explain the typical characteristics of private equity, including the structure of private equity partnerships, the historical returns generated from private equity investing, and the common investment categories of venture capital, growth capital and leveraged buyouts.

Our attention then turns to the specifics of the UK listed private equity sector – with an overview of the various funds available, including some of the advantages of investing in these funds and the fee structures associated with them. Subsequently, we introduce the key risks in private equity investing – using our common framework which looks at (i) business risks (ii) financial risks and (iii) valuation risks to better inform readers.

Interest rates play a crucial role in capital market returns – with lower interest rates offering a potential boost to asset prices, while higher interest rates can often weigh on asset prices – and have come into focus recently due to rising interest rates in developed countries, following an extended period of ultra-low rates. Understanding the role interest rates play in valuing assets is fundamental for any investor, and we look to educate the reader in that regard.

By the end of this booklet the reader will have a deeper understanding of private equity investing. For those interested in investing in private equity markets, we hope that with an understanding of the UK listed private equity universe and the key risks it entails, you can make more informed investment decisions and can increase the odds of generating attractive investment returns.

Jonathan Yates
March 2023

Background

Modern private equity markets date back to 1946 with the founding of two venture capital firms, J.H. Whitney & Company and American Research & Development Corp., which was founded by Georges Doriot, known as the "father of venture capitalism". Generally, investments tended to be small and were focused on starting and expanding companies. The first private equity fund structure, known more commonly in the industry as a partnership, was introduced in the 1960s.

However, it was not until the 1980s that we saw the first boom in private equity in an era characterised by "corporate raiders" and hostile takeovers, including the $25 billion buyout of RJR Nabisco by KKR which was made famous by the book, *Barbarians at the Gate*.[1] Towards the end of the decade, several other large buyouts ended in bankruptcy.

Venture capital funding, a sub-category of private equity, played a role in fuelling the dot-com bubble in the late 1990s – backing many of the highest profile technology companies at that time such as Amazon, eBay and Yahoo!. As the overvalued technology market peaked and subsequently collapsed, venture capital firms were forced to write down investments and were also selling investments in the secondary market at steep discounts in an effort to raise liquidity. Ultimately, the venture capital market halved in size between 2001 and 2003.

A resurgence in private equity began in the mid-2000s, often referred to as 'the Golden Age of Private Equity', with the continuous breaking of records (mainly deal size) between 2003 and 2007. A total of 654 companies were

---

[1] *Barbarians at the Gate: The Fall of RJR Nabisco*, Bryan Burroughs & John Helyar, Harper & Row, 1989.

bought in the US by private equity firms in 2006 alone, while the total value of leveraged buyouts, the most common investment category in private equity, in that year amounted to $804 billion globally. Some high-profile buyouts of that era included Harrah's Entertainment, the owner of casino resorts in Las Vegas, and Chrysler, the US automobile manufacturer. However, no market was immune to the Global Financial Crisis in 2008 and with its significant use of leverage, private equity was once again on its knees – as activity dried up and many investments were written down to zero.

As the scars started to heal at the turn of the decade, private equity transactions began to pick up once again with a significant amount of capital flowing into the industry, aided by an ultra-low interest rate environment. With the exception of a brief blip during the Covid-19 pandemic in 2020, deal volumes remained strong up to the end of 2021 – with buyouts worth $1.1 trillion in 2021 passing the previous peak set in 2006.

Through the boom-and-bust cycles, private equity markets have been growing strongly over the last two decades but are still only a fraction of total global equity markets. While institutional investors have doubled their allocation of assets to private equity investments over the last decade, retail investors are only beginning to allocate assets towards private equity which, to some degree, reflects the difficultly in accessing the market.

What is Private Equity?

Today, the global private capital markets are estimated to be around $9.8 trillion in size – which covers private investments in companies (equity), real estate, infrastructure, natural resources and debt. In this booklet we focus on private equity, which is the largest of the private markets, with *circa* $6.3 trillion of assets under management at the end of 2021. This compares to public equity markets which are valued at over $100 trillion globally.

The largest private equity firms in the world are mostly US based and include Blackstone, Carlyle Group, KKR, Apollo Global, TPG Capital and Bain Capital. In Europe, well-known private equity houses include EQT Infrastructure, 3i Group, CVC Capital Partners, Apax Partners, Permira and Partners Group.

Private equity broadly refers to investments that are made in companies that are not publicly listed on a stock exchange, either through ownership of the company or an interest in the entity. Investors are attracted to private equity as it offers the potential for higher returns by providing them access to specialised managers with a long-term focus who take stakes in private companies with the aim of generating above average returns over time.

General partners (private equity firms) invest capital with the aim of improving the performance of these companies and reselling them at a higher value. General partners adopt a range of measures, which are company specific, to improve these companies, including operational improvements, enabling investment for the future, strengthening management teams, and making better use of the company's balance sheet. Because these companies are not publicly listed, the managers do not have to be concerned about meeting quarterly targets or short-term share price gyrations which is common with publicly listed companies – allowing for a more long-term focus.

Typically, private equity investments are structured through a partnership where a general partner oversees investments from limited partners in a fund-like vehicle – typically making 10 to 20 investments in individual private companies over the life of the partnership. The majority of private equity partnerships are referred to as 'blind pools' where the actual investments are not specified prior to limited partners making commitments, although the general partner will describe the types of investments expected to be made. Limited partners can include hedge funds, pension funds, university endowments, foundations and/or wealthy individuals.

Investors commit a certain amount of capital up front which can be drawn down – typically over three to five years – by the general partner for investment, which can come at any stage and is dependent on the investment opportunities available at any given time. The minimum investment from any one fund/individual into the partnership is relatively high and can range anywhere between $250,000 to $25 million. In other words, investors have to lock up a certain portion of their capital to ensure they can provide the capital when it is called upon by the general partner.

The average investment period in a company tends to be between three and seven years dependent on the specific situation and general partners will use a number of different strategies when exiting investments including:

- **Trade sales**: The private company is sold to another suitable company, with the acquirer often having a strategic motive for the business which complements its existing businesses. The acquirer tends to pay a premium, as a result.

- **Secondary buyouts**: The company is sold to another private equity firm. Reasons may include the company needing further investment which the current owner cannot meet, or the private equity firm may believe another firm's expertise is better suited for growing the business going forward.

- **Initial Public Offering (IPO)**: The company is listed on a stock exchange, with the shares of the company offered to the public in a new stock issuance for the first time.

The proceeds from these exits are then returned to the limited partners based on pre-agreed terms. Proceeds tend not to be re-invested, so these funds (or partnerships) are self-liquidating with the lifespan of these funds generally being 10 to 12 years. Of course, not all investments are successful and a less than favourable exit strategy would be a liquidation of the company.

A standard compensation (or fee) structure for partnerships has limited partners paying an annual management fee of 1% to 2% and a performance fee, which is more commonly referred to as 'carried interest' in the industry, typically representing up to 20% of the profits of the partnership. This performance fee also commonly includes an annual hurdle rate of return of 8%.[2]

During the early years of an investment in private equity, an investor's net investment return can be negative for some time, referred to in the industry as the J-curve effect. This reflects the fact that an investor's capital is committed at the outset and management fees are continuously being paid to general partners. It is not until investments in companies begin to be realised (and hopefully successfully) that an investor will start to see positive returns on his/her investment in the partnership.

So, with capital locked up for a significant amount of time and the higher fee structure associated with gaining access to high-quality private equity

---

[2]   The 20% performance fee is earned only after the investors have received a return of 8% per annum.

managers, investors would naturally expect these private equity investments to add significant value. And the evidence does point to private equity investing providing higher returns to investors than public equity markets. Cambridge Associates, the US-based financial services company, provides a US Private Equity Index[3] which has delivered annual returns of 14.4% over a 36-year period to end June 2022, outperforming the 10.3% annual total return (dividends reinvested) from the S&P 500 Index over this period.

Chart 1: Cambridge Associates US Private Equity Index vs S&P 500 Total Return Index: Value of $100 Invested in March 1986

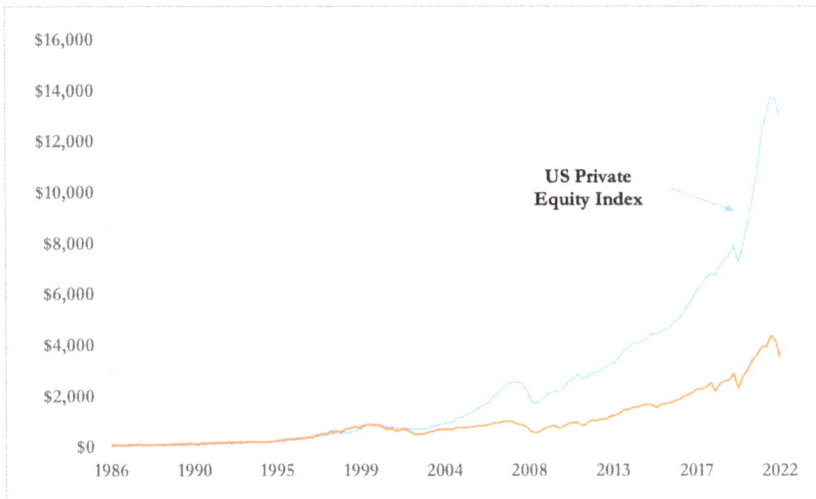

Source: Cambridge Associates and Bloomberg.

Types of Private Equity

Private equity covers a wide breadth and managers will often look to focus on (and specialise in) a certain category of private equity. Common investment categories within the private equity space include:

---

[3]   An index calculated based on data compiled from over 2,000 private equity funds, including fully liquidated partnerships. All returns are net of fees, expenses and carried interest.

- **Venture Capital (VC)**: Investments in companies that are early in their life cycle (start-ups) which tend to be focused on new technologies, new marketing concepts or new products that don't have a proven track record. VC is regarded as higher risk but with the potential for high rewards (returns) – a rule of thumb is that for every 10 start-ups, three to four will fail.

- **Growth Capital:** Typically, minority investments in companies which are relatively mature and need additional capital investment to fuel future growth through entering new markets or making large acquisitions.

- **Leveraged Buyouts (LBO):** An investment which acquires a majority stake in a business and uses a significant amount of debt (leverage) to help finance the acquisition. Leveraged buyouts tend to be in mature companies that are generating positive cash flow.

- **Other:** Smaller categories of private equity include royalty funds and merchant banking.

Fund of fund structures are also common in private equity whereby a fund invests in several other private equity partnerships with the primary focus of allocating capital to high quality managers who are identifying attractive investment opportunities. Fund of funds come with many advantages such as improved diversification and access to the top performing funds/managers. However, these fund structures come with higher fees as the fund must also pay fees on the underlying private equity funds it invests in which are passed on to investors.

Leveraged buyout is the most common form of private equity. In 2021, buyouts accounted for roughly half of global private equity fundraising while venture capital represented about 25% to 30%. Growth capital was a further *circa* 20%, with other forms of private equity representing a much smaller proportion of total fundraising. The pattern of annual fundraising has been similar over the 12 years from 2010 to 2021 – as highlighted in ***Chart 2***.

Chart 2: Global Private Equity Fundraising ($ billions)

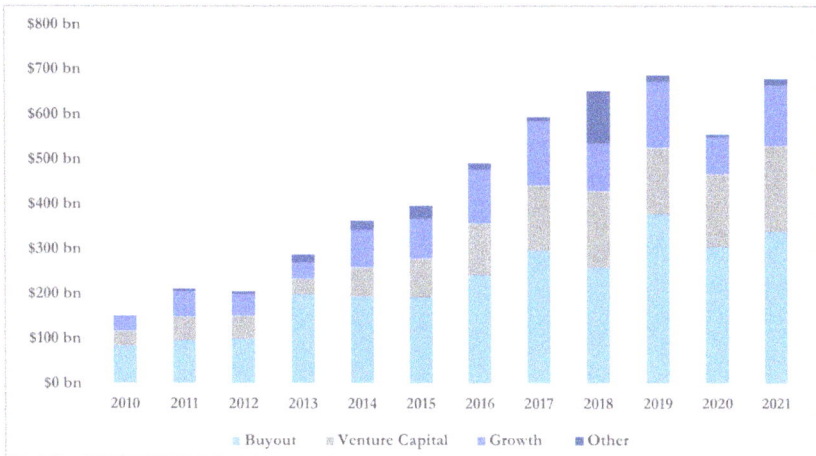

Source: Preqin.

For institutional investors (as opposed to retail investors) allocating capital to private equity, there are three common approaches when looking to access the asset class:

- **Primary fund investments**: The investor makes the initial commitments to the fund and the manager begins to invest the proceeds which are returned to investors as the companies are sold. Annualised returns of 15%+ are expected by investors and the typical lifespan of the investment is 10 to 12 years.

- **Secondary investments**: The purchase of an existing investment in a private equity fund/partnership, typically at a discount to net asset value. The fund is already invested, so there is greater visibility over the portfolio with expected returns of 12% to 15% annually over a period of two to seven years.

- **Co-investments:** A direct investment in a company alongside the fund manager which tends to arise when a fund has insufficient capital to purchase a company so limited partners are given the opportunity to increase their position. These investments come with reduced fees for the institutional investor and returns can be as high as 30% annually over a period of four to seven years.

UK Listed Private Equity Vehicles – A sub-sector of the Market

While traditional private equity investments, through limited partnerships, come with many attractions, the reality is that they can be difficult to access for ordinary/retail investors. A clear hurdle for many is the size of the minimum investment, while capital is also locked up for an extended period of time. Even if an investor has the capital and time commitment, it is often the case that the best managers in private equity are closed to new investors. In addition, diversification often requires an allocation to multiple private equity managers, further increasing the capital requirement and costs.

The difficulty for an investor who is not an expert in the space is that he/she does not have the required experience or expertise in particular business sectors and may not have a full understanding of how to value the investment opportunities. And, in many cases, these investment opportunities are being offered by product sellers (intermediaries, stockbrokers, etc.) who are getting paid to raise the money for the business or private equity partnership, so they will be mostly inclined to give the opportunity a favourable review.

However, there exists an investment universe to overcome these challenges. The UK listed private equity sector, a sub-sector of the private equity market, provides liquid investment funds which are diversified and offer investors exposure to specialised managers and the long-term growth trends in private equity with no lock-up periods or minimum size of investment. An investor with a small sum of capital can gain exposure to some of the highest-quality private equity managers, such as Pantheon International, HarbourVest Global, HgCapital Trust and Princess Private Equity, amongst others.

Table 1 provides a list of some of the investment funds in the universe which we will be referring to both collectively and individually throughout this booklet – six funds that invest directly in private companies and five that are predominantly fund of funds structures. There are also a number of pure-play Venture/ Growth focused funds listed in the UK which we will not discuss, so this is not an exhaustive list. (**Note:** these investment vehicles are either investment trusts or investment holding companies. For simplicity, we will refer to them collectively as funds. For a definition of these terms, please refer to the *Glossary* at the end of this booklet.)

Table 1: Selected Universe of UK Listed Private Equity Funds

	Ticker
Direct	
3i Group	III LN
Apax Global Alpha	APAX LN
HgCapital Trust	HGT LN
NB Private Equity	NBPE LN
Oakley Capital	OCI LN
Princess Private Equity	PEY LN
Fund of Funds	
Abrdn Private Equity Opportunities	APEO LN
CT Private Equity	CTPE LN
HarbourVest Global	HVPE LN
ICG Enterprise Trust	ICGT LN
Pantheon International	PIN LN

Source: Company Reports and Bloomberg.

Many of these funds were launched by large, well-known private equity houses that run many unlisted private equity funds (*i.e.* not listed on the stock exchange). For example, Princess Private Equity is managed by Partners Group, a Swiss-based global asset management company with $131 billion under management across private equity, credit, real estate and infrastructure investments. In this case, the Princess Private Equity fund listed on the London Stock Exchange is just a small part of Partners Group's overall private equity business but is one that smaller retail investors can access.

These are closed-ended fund structures which are listed on the London Stock Exchange. Initially, the funds issue a fixed number of shares through an IPO with the raised capital used for initial investments in private equity opportunities identified by the manager. The share prices of listed private equity funds are then priced on a daily basis like any publicly listed company and can be bought and sold on the stock exchange at any time. However, the underlying investment portfolio, referred to as the fund's net asset value (NAV), is only valued on a periodic basis (bi-annually or quarterly). As a result, the fund's share price can from time to time deviate significantly from the fund's underlying net asset value.

These funds value their investments based on the International Private Equity Valuations (IPEV) guidelines which set out recommendations intended for best practices on the valuation of private equity investments. The objective is for the funds to report fair values using valuation techniques such as discounted cash flow models, a revenue or earnings multiple approach, an industry valuation benchmark approach or a replacement cost approach, among others.

Unlike traditional private equity funds/partnerships which have a fixed life span and tend to close after 10 to 12 years, these listed private equity vehicles reinvest the capital proceeds from selling companies within their private equity portfolio into new opportunities – benefiting investors with tax-free compounding returns.

Compared to their non-listed private equity counterparts, these listed vehicles come with a number of advantages, including:

- No minimum investment requirement, which makes these funds accessible to all investor types including small retail investors with small investment portfolios.

- With the closed-ended structure and the shares trading daily, this provides liquidity for investors who can enter and exit these funds at any stage with no lock-up periods.

- While private equity partnerships tend to have a lifespan of 10 to 12 years, these funds have no fixed life as investment proceeds are reinvested. This has an added benefit for the fund manager who can take a truly long-term approach to investing.

- These funds are run by top quality managers with an experienced investment team, who have worked in private equity markets for many years.

- These funds are already invested in a diversified portfolio of companies, so investors can get an understanding of the type of funds they are investing in prior to making a capital commitment.

- As the proceeds are reinvested in new opportunities, the sale of an investment by the manager does not trigger a tax event for an investor and he/she is only subject to tax when the shares are sold or, in the case of some of the funds in the universe, when a dividend is paid out to investors. In addition, gains on the sale of shares of these funds are subject to capital gains tax, as opposed to income tax.

- The funds are also subject to certain reporting requirements and corporate governance rules, so a certain level of transparency is given to investors. Annual and interim reports are released while the managers engage through analyst calls and investor updates throughout the year.

Fee Structures

The fee structures in the UK listed private equity space differ per fund but they do tend to have some commonalities. In general, the fees on these funds are higher than the fees paid for investing in funds that invest in a portfolio of publicly listed companies. A base fee is charged as a percentage of net assets, while a performance fee is also levied based on some annual hurdle rate of return. Other costs can include borrowing costs, portfolio transaction costs and other administrative costs.

Along with these costs, a fund of funds structure also has the added cost of having to pay fees to the funds in which it invests, often the standard 1% to 2% management fee on assets and a 20% fee on any outperformance which we discussed previously.

To help provide a better understanding of the fees investors can expect when investing in these funds we will highlight two examples of fee structures: Princess Private Equity, a direct investment fund and Pantheon International, predominantly a fund of funds.

According to Princess Private Equity's Key Information Document[4] total annual costs in the fund amount to 5.51%. Portfolio transaction costs account for 0.10%, the annual management fee is 1.50% of NAV, and other ongoing costs account for 0.81% (*e.g.*, admin fees, borrowing costs, service fees), while the performance fee is quoted as 2.31%. The performance fee is levied on

---

[4]   A two-page document which aims to provide critical information to investors about a fund, highlighting the key risks and costs for investors in the fund.

different investment types: (i) a 15% performance fee per direct investments; (ii) a 10% performance fee per secondary investment; and (iii) no performance fee on primary investments. Performance fees are subject to an 8% annual performance hurdle. The fee is levied per investment rather than at the fund level.

For Pantheon International, the fund charges a management fee of 1.5% *per annum* on the value of assets up to £150 million and 1% *per annum* on the value of assets above £150 million. The group also has an annual performance fee of 5% on any outperformance greater than 10% growth on the previous year-end NAV – which also includes a high-water mark.[5] As a fund of funds, the trust also pays fees to the funds in which it invests. These fees, however, aren't disclosed in the Annual Report and can only be estimated by the investment manager. As highlighted previously, these are often a 1% to 2% management fee on assets and a 20% fee on any outperformance. Overall, on a look-through basis, then, investors in Pantheon International can expect to pay total management fees of up to 3% to 4% *per annum* before accounting for performance fees which could add over 2% to costs.

Overall, while these fees are typical of private equity funds, they are nonetheless expensive. That said, an analysis of the performance of these funds is done on a net-of-fees basis and, as we will highlight in this booklet, the long-term track record of net asset value growth (after all costs) has been strong for these funds despite the high costs borne by investors in private equity.

Appendix 1 provides a breakdown of the fee structures for the UK listed private equity universe as per each fund's Key Information Document highlighted in *Table 1*.

Taxation of Listed Private Equity Vehicles

As we outlined previously, listed private equity vehicles are either investment trusts or investment holding companies. Investment holding companies are taxed like regular stock exchange listed companies, so these investments fall under the capital gains tax regime.

---

5   A high-water mark is the highest level in value the NAV has reached. To earn a performance fee, the fund must first surpass this high-water mark.

While investment trusts are not specifically dealt with by the Irish Revenue authorities, the existence of Real Estate Investment Trust (REIT) legislation in Ireland suggests that the two structures should be treated similarly. REITs in Ireland are also taxed under the capital gains tax regime.

So, under the capital gains tax regime in Ireland, capital gains are taxed at 33%, dividend income at your marginal rate of tax and losses can be offset against gains. In addition, gains are only taxed when crystallised.

In Ireland, investors may be restricted from trading investment trust vehicles in Personal Retirement Saving Accounts (PRSAs), reflecting restrictions due to performance and/or incidental fees charged by these vehicles. Investors looking for more information on this issue should contact their broker. However, no such restrictions apply to personal, corporate or Approved Retirement Fund (ARF) accounts.

2: ANALYSING THE RISKS IN LISTED PRIVATE EQUITY

At GillenMarkets we adopt a common framework for assessing the risks in companies and the risk assessment we apply to private equity investing is no different. In the following sections we will discuss these risks in detail, which can be broken down into business, financial and valuation risks:

- **Business risk** is the risk that the business model has deteriorated and that past levels of profitability are unlikely to be achieved again in the future. These risks can be both internal and external and some examples of factors that might impact business profitability include poor management, increased competition, changing preferences of its customers, changes in government policy and obsolescence due to technological advances.

- **Financial risk** is the risk of adopting inappropriate financial and debt levels that expose companies to failure, particularly in a more difficult market environment, potentially leading to substantial permanent losses for an investor. A company that can no longer pay down debt or service its interest payments runs the risk of bankruptcy.

- **Valuation risk** is the risk of an investor overpaying for an asset, even if the asset is of high quality, which will reduce future returns. We have seen countless examples throughout history when investors have disregarded valuations and have been willing to pay any price for an asset. An example we have used on many occasions is Coca-Cola in the late 1990s. Its share price peaked in mid-1998 and did not return to this level for another 18 years. The issue for Coca-Cola was not a deterioration of its business as earnings continued to grow over this period, but the fact that investors were willing to pay any price for the shares in the late 1990s – with some paying over 55 times earnings at the peak in 1998.

We will address each of these risks individually in the following sections.

Business Risk

When investing in investment funds as opposed to single companies, how one looks at business risk is somewhat different. Nonetheless, the fund is investing in a basket of companies so business risk still applies but an investor's focus is more on the manager. The aim is to invest in a manager who he/she believes is implementing a consistent investment strategy and is investing in a portfolio of companies where the manager understands and accounts for the key business risks associated with the underlying companies and sectors in which they operate. So, business risks in listed private equity funds are much lower compared to investing in single company opportunities.

In this section we will look at some of the differences and similarities between the investment approaches of the funds in the UK listed private equity universe. We will also take a look at the growth track record for private equity – both in terms of the underlying companies for the funds and the net asset value returns generated by these funds since 1999. Finally, we will look at the role that declining interest rates have played in private equity returns over the last decade or so.

Investment Approaches

As we highlighted previously, the funds are often managed by larger private equity firms which manage many non-listed private equity funds along with other private funds in credit, real estate and infrastructure. The investment approaches of these private equity firms are, in most cases, mirrored in the listed fund's approach and a key aspect of private equity is that managers aim to specialise in a certain investment type, sector, geography, etc. where the manager can apply specific expertise and knowledge.

Table 2 provides a brief summary of each of the fund's investment strategy, along with their focus in terms of geographic location for investments. As the table highlights, the funds investing directly are focused on identifying companies with specific characteristics and/or are operating in specific sectors, characterised by certain themes which, in turn, are driving above average growth within these markets.

Table 2: Private Equity Fund Strategy Summary

	Strategy Summary	Geography
Direct		
3i Group	Technology, Consumer and Healthcare along with Infrastructure investments	Europe
Apax Global Alpha	Tech & Telco, Services, Healthcare and Consumer	Global
HgCapital Trust	Technology investments, primarily software and service companies	Europe, UK, North America
NB Private Equity	Companies that are expected to benefit from long-term structural growth trends	North America, Europe
Oakley Capital	Profitable, high-growth businesses across Tech, Consumer and Education	Germany, Austria, Switzerland
Princess Private Equity	High-quality small and mid-cap companies	Global
Fund of Funds		
Abrdn Private Equity Opportunities	Managers investing in mature, cash-generative companies	Europe
CT Private Equity	Managers with a proven track record of excellent absolute returns	UK, Europe
HarbourVest Global	Managers investing in high-quality companies with strong balance sheets	Global
ICG Enterprise Trust	Managers investing in profitable, cash-generative companies	Global
Pantheon International	High quality managers and companies benefiting from technology and digitisation	Global

Source: Company filings.

The private equity model has changed significantly from the early days of the 1980s when the focus was mainly on buying well-run companies with good management teams already in place and creating value through financial engineering, typically leveraging the company and cutting costs. While leverage remains a key tool of the model, over the last decade or so there has been a shift in focus towards improving the operations of a company and taking a buy-and-build approach to create significant value for investors. Management teams are often replaced or improved with industry experts, while investment through acquisitions, capital expenditure and R & D has also increased to fuel growth.

For fund of funds, the focus is on investing in funds run by high quality managers which are adopting a consistent investment approach, identifying companies with certain characteristics operating in growth markets. In some cases, these funds of funds are also making (direct) co-investments which stem from building good relationships with managers which, from time to time, offer these co-investment opportunities.

Table 3: Fund Investment Type

Investment Type	
Direct	
3i Group	82% Buyout, 18% Infrastructure
Apax Global Alpha	75% Buyout, 23% Debt, 2% Other
HgCapital Trust	100% Buyout
NB Private Equity	92% Buyout, 8% Other
Oakley Capital	100% Buyout
Princess Private Equity	Buyout 89%, Venture 3%, Special Situations 8%
Fund of Funds	
Abrdn Private Equity Opportunities	Buyout 100%
CT Private Equity	Buyout 96%, Venture/Growth 4%
HarbourVest Global	Buyout 56%, Venture/Growth 33%, Other 11%
ICG Enterprise Trust	Buyout 97%, Other 3%
Pantheon International	Buyout 65%, Venture/Growth 28%, Special Situations 7%

Source: Company filings.

Similar to the broader private equity market, buyouts are the main investment category across this sub-universe of the market, particularly for the direct investment funds, and in some cases the only investment type. For some of the funds of funds, there is also exposure to other areas of private capital markets. As we can see from *Table 3*, HarbourVest Global has 33% of its net assets invested in Venture Capital and Growth-type investment opportunities.

Sector Exposure

An overarching theme of the investment approaches of these private equity funds is that they look to avoid cyclical areas of the market such as energy, focusing more on companies operating in sectors that tend to be resilient and less cyclical but offer the potential for robust growth over the medium to long-term. In general, managers are looking for profitable companies that are generating strong and consistent cash flows but also have strong balance sheets to support the company through challenging economic environments. This approach lends itself more to sectors such as technology, healthcare and consumer staples/discretionary/services.

Among the funds in the universe is HgCapital Trust which looks to specialise in investing in software and services companies in the technology sector and focuses on eight core end markets within the broader tech space. In recent years, Pantheon International has been increasing its investments in new economy companies with technology, consumer and healthcare now accounting for over 60% of the portfolio.

Growth Track Record – Underlying Portfolio Holdings

Since the dawn of time, people have traded with each other and, from trade, businesses develop. The natural forces of trade, innovation and specialisation lead to improvements in productivity, which along with a growing population leads to growth in the economy. So, economic growth is driven principally by business over time. Investing in businesses carries risk, however, so businesses must be valued in a way that ensures the investor or businessmen can obtain a return that is higher than non-risk assets such as bank deposits.

While the investment funds discussed previously take different approaches to private equity investing in terms of investment style, company characteristics, geography, sectors, etc., the ultimate goal remains constant throughout – the managers aim to acquire companies at a certain price, improve the companies' performance, grow their earnings over time, and eventually sell these companies for a profit at a future date.

Through various measures – operational improvements, providing investment for future growth through acquisitions or investing to improve the existing business, strengthening management teams and/or efficiently managing a company's balance sheet – the goal is to grow the business through increasing revenues and, thus, profits. Profits, and the ability to continue to grow these profits over time and translate them into cash flow, is how investors ultimately value investments.

Warren Buffett, chairman and CEO of Berkshire Hathaway, often simplifies valuing an investment with the following quote:

"The value of any stock, bond or business today is determined by the cash inflows and outflows — discounted at an appropriate interest rate — that can be expected to occur during the remaining life of the asset."

Evidence points to these funds investing in companies that are growing strongly. *Table 4* provides a breakdown of the average annual revenue and profit[6] growth for companies within the portfolio. The figures are based on disclosures from the funds and, in some cases, funds do not provide any growth figures for the underlying portfolios. In addition, the figures are generally based on an average of a sample of the portfolio – top 20 holdings, top 30 holdings, or top 50 holdings and can account for anywhere between 30% and 70% of the fund's net assets. Overall, the goal is to provide a snapshot of the underlying growth being generated by these companies.

As the table highlights, underlying growth in the portfolios has been strong – with companies, on average, growing revenues at double digit (or close to) annual rates over the last 10 years while annual EBITDA growth has been even higher and, in some cases, close to 20%. A sample of companies in HgCapital Trust's portfolio, for example, grew EBITDA by 19.2% compound *per annum*, on average, between 2012 and 2021 – with its focus on technology companies benefiting the group in recent years.

---

[6]   Profit figures are EBITDA – see **Glossary** for description.

Table 4: Underlying Portfolio Growth

10-Year Compound *per annum*		
	Revenue	EBITDA
3i Group	25.2%	25.3%
Apax Global Alpha*	12.5%	18.4%
HgCapital Trust	16.0%	19.2%
NB Private Equity	9.6%	15.0%
Princess Private Equity	11.0%	13.4%
HarbourVest Global**	-	12.9%
ICG Enterprise Trust	11.3%	14.6%
Pantheon International	15.1%	15.6%

* *7-year annual growth rate.*
** *5-year annual growth rate.*

Source: Company filings.

Of course, as always is the case, past performance is not indicative of future performance. However, the above table does provide some confidence that, on average, these funds are investing in good quality companies that are delivering above average growth.

The ability of private equity managers, along with the management teams of each company, to deliver this underlying company growth is then reflected in the valuation of the fund's net asset value. As outlined previously, the valuation of private equity investments at these firms is carried in accordance with International Private Equity Valuations guidelines. While this does provide a standard framework for valuation and an approximation of fair value, net asset values are ultimately estimates of company value.

The value of something is determined by what another buyer is willing to pay for it. So, looking at realisations – the sale of investments by private equity firms – is helpful. And evidence would not only justify the valuations placed on these assets by firms but, in many cases, indicate that the valuations of companies in these portfolios are being carried by these funds at conservative levels. In other words, private equity firms are consistently conservative in their valuations.

Some of the funds in the UK listed private equity universe report the average uplift to the carrying value[7] from realisations (disposals) in the reporting period – with uplifts provided in annual reports and based on valuations at the previous year end or the most recent valuation update. Four of the funds in question have reported figures on an annual basis over the last 10 years. As **Table 5** highlights, the average uplift to carrying value has been consistently strong for all four funds.

Table 5: Average Uplift to Carrying Value

	2012	2013	2014	2015	2016	2017	2018	2019	2020	2021
HgCapital Trust	73%	19%	54%	40%	28%	63%	43%	10%	36%	45%
ICG Enterprise Trust	52%	36%	35%	22%	24%	40%	35%	37%	31%	36%
NB Private Equity	10%	5%	22%	5%	22%	36%	41%	22%	30%	83%
Pantheon International	36%	26%	25%	31%	34%	35%	22%	36%	28%	26%

Source: Company filings.

So, tying it all together, the key performance indicator for these funds is their ability to grow their net asset values over time. Over the long-term, the track record of the UK listed private equity space is strong – see **Chart 3**.

The chart highlights the net asset value total return performance of the UK listed private equity universe (ex 3i Group) in sterling terms since 1999 and compares it with the returns from the MSCI All Country World Index on a total return basis over the same period. Over the 20-year+ period from end of 1999 to today, the UK listed private equity space has delivered NAV growth on a total return basis of 8.4% compound *per annum* which compares to a 6.6% compound *per annum* total return for the MSCI All Country World Index.

---

[7] The percentage by which the selling price was above the carrying value of an investment on the balance sheet.

Chart 3: UK Listed Private Equity (ex 3i Group) NAV Total Return *vs* MSCI AC World Index

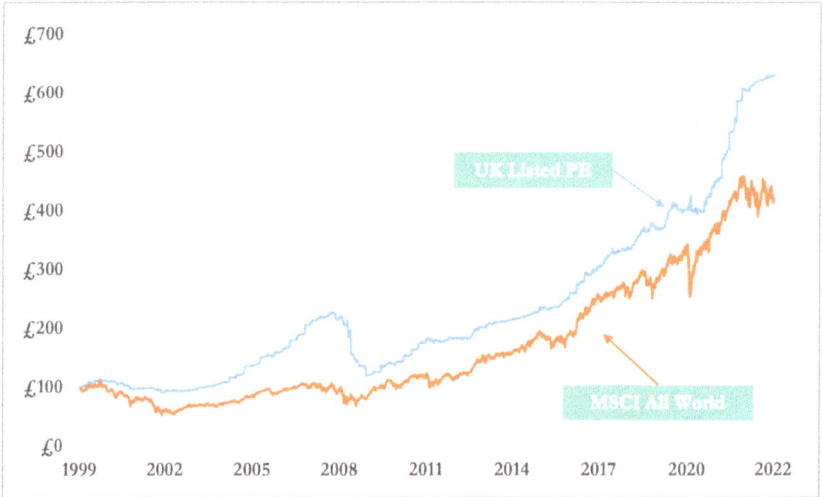

Source: DataStream.

At the end of this booklet, we provide individual profiles for three of the funds in the universe – HgCapital Trust, Pantheon International and Princess Private Equity. HgCapital Trust and Pantheon International have strongly outperformed the FTSE All-World Index since 1995, while Princess Private Equity's performance has been in line with the index since inception in 2007.

The Role of Declining Interest Rates

Developed markets have gone on a 41-year run of declining interest rates and the extent of the declines is highlighted in ***Chart 4*** – the yield (or interest rate) on US 10-Year Government Bonds since 1968.

Chart 4: US 10-Year Government Bond Yield

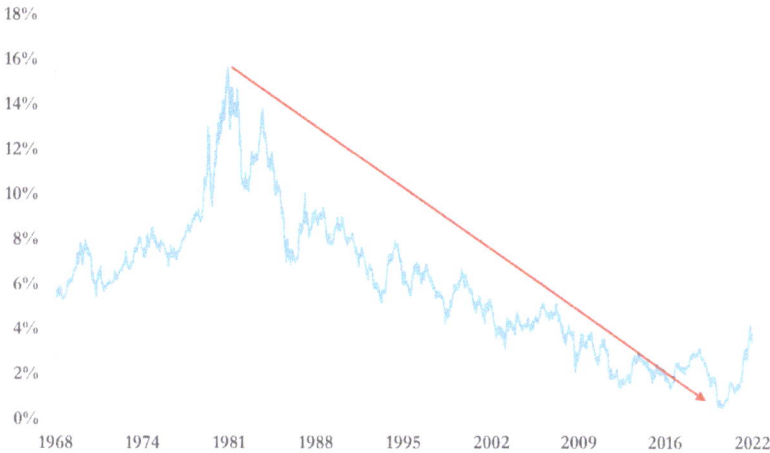

Source: Bloomberg.

During the period between the end of the Global Financial Crisis in 2009 to the end of 2021 we have seen a period of ultra-low interest rates – with negative interest rates in some major countries, such as Germany.

Declining interest rates (as represented by the government bond yield in the chart) have played a significant role in capital markets' returns since the 1980s. To help assist the reader in understanding the key role that interest rates have in the valuation of an asset, we will provide the following example.

The owner of a small retail shop earns €50,000 annually after tax and such shops in the area are selling for 10 times earnings as a rule of thumb. The owner plans to sell the shop and retire in five years' time. If bank deposit rates are 6%, what value might you place on this business today? If there are no risks to the expected €750k of cash flows, made up of the €50k annual profits and a lump-sum of €500k at the end of the 5-year period, the answer is €584k.

Table 6: Valuing an Asset (i)

Year	Cash Flows	Discounted @ 6%
1	€50,000	€47,170
2	€50,000	€44,500
3	€50,000	€41,981
4	€50,000	€39,605
5	€550,000	€410,992
Total	€750,000	€584,248

Source: GillenMarkets.

To get to this figure, we take the initial €50k profits expected at the end of year 1. If interest rates are 6%, that €50k is worth €47.17k to you now because €47.17k placed on deposit today earning 6% will compound to €50k in one year's time. As **Table 6** outlines, the entire €750k of cash flows you expect to receive over the five years are worth €584k today calculated in the same way.

Table 7: Valuing an Asset (ii)

Business Value	Interest Rates
€584,248	6.0%
€608,237	5.0%
€633,555	4.0%
€660,290	3.0%
€688,538	2.0%
€718,404	1.0%

Source: GillenMarkets.

Table 7 provides a breakdown of the value of the business at various interest rates all calculated in the same way as the example. So, if bank deposits rates were 3% today that would place a higher value on the shop of €660k today. The basic message is clear: the lower interest rates are, the higher the value of the business today. At lower interest rates, you need to place progressively more monies on deposit to compound to €750k in the time given. The rationale for this is that, if you can get the same return from monies placed on deposit with a bank, what would entice you to pay any more for this business today?

For example, if interest rates were 4% and you had €633.5k to invest, you would compound your monies to €750k after five years. In reverse, if you were due to receive a total of €750k over a 5-year period and interest rates were 4% today, what would entice you to pay more than the €633.5k today for those cash flows? Very little, if you are a rational investor!

Of course, when we value the shop like this, we are assuming no risk to the shop's cash flows over the next five years. In reality, there would be plenty of risks – the risk that a competitor starts up a new shop down the road or the risk that demand for what the shop is selling goes online. For simplicity, we have not brought these considerations into our example. However, the example shows the key role of interest rates in the valuation of an asset.

Going back to Warren Buffett's quote on the valuation of a business being the value of future cash flows discounted at an appropriate interest rate, this 'appropriate' interest rate has been in decline for many years. And the valuation of a private equity investment is no different. In simple terms, the value of a fund's net asset value is just the collective value of the underlying businesses within the portfolio. As a result, declining interest rates have played a key role in increasing the valuations placed on these assets in recent years.

Given the extensive use of leverage in private equity deals, an ultra-low interest rate environment has provided a surplus of capital for private equity firms at extremely low cost (interest payments) leading to a booming period for private equity deals. For example, global deal count and deal volume reached 14,686 and $2.04 trillion, respectively, in 2021, well above the previous peak of *circa* 7,500 deal sand $1.4 trillion in 2007. In other words, there has been too much capital chasing too few deals, which increases the price (or value) of these assets even further.

Financial Risk

When analysing the financial risk within the UK listed private equity space, it is important to examine it from two angles:

- The underlying debt levels being applied by private equity companies – on a market level and in the portfolios of the funds in the universe.

- The funds in the universe in terms of gearing adopted at a fund level, along with their liquidity resources and total future commitments it has made to private equity partnerships which could be called upon in the near future.

Chart 5: Median Debt-to-EBITDA ratio in Private Equity Market 2007 – 2021

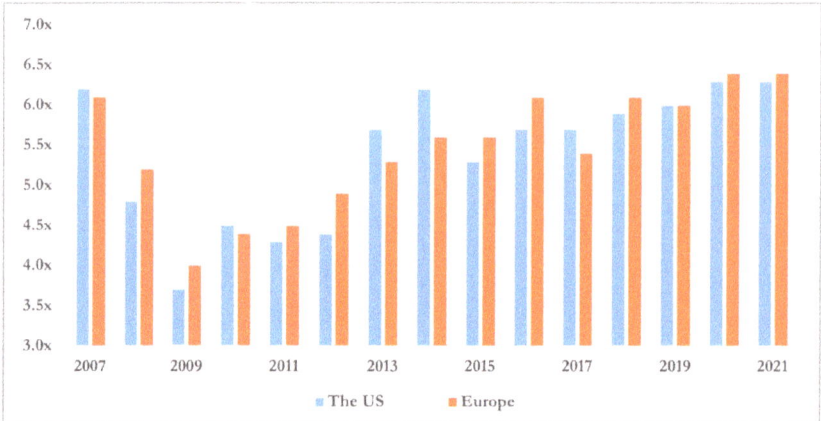

Source: Pitchbook.

Chart 5 provides a breakdown of the median debt-to-EBITDA ratio for the US and European private equity markets between 2007 and 2021. Data from different sources for private equity markets differs somewhat, most likely reflecting sample size, calculation method, area of focus. etc. The data we use in the chart is sourced from Pitchbook, a credible data and research company which is owned by MorningStar and is focused on covering private capital markets including venture capital, private equity and M&A transactions.

As the chart highlights, the ratios for both the US and European markets at the last peak in 2007 were above 6x. As outlined in the previous section, declining interest rates and easy access to credit over the last decade or so have provided a supportive backdrop for borrowing. As a result, the debt-to-EBITDA ratios for the private equity market have been steadily rising from the lows of below 4x in 2009, and debt levels are now back near the peak levels seen in 2007.

Chart 6: Debt-to-EBITDA Ratios for Underlying Portfolios

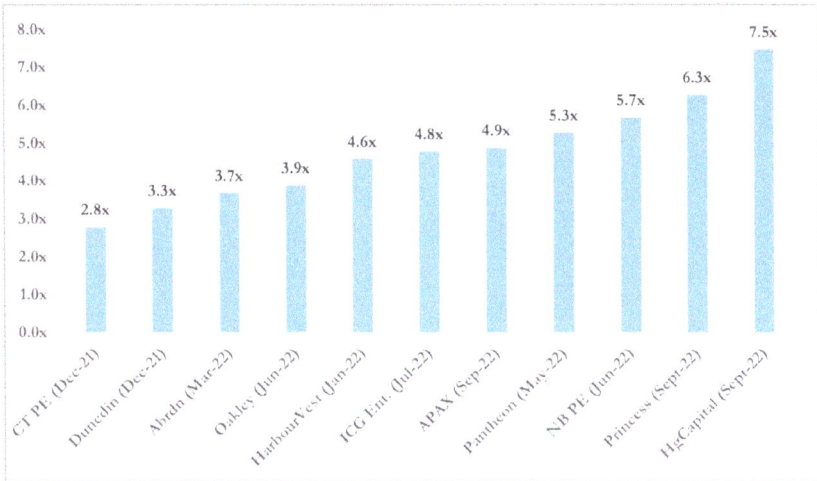

Source: Most Recent Company Filings

In **Chart 6**, we highlight the debt-to-EBITDA ratio for the underlying portfolios of the funds in the universe at the most recently reported date. Generally, these funds report the average figure for a sample of the portfolio – which can be based on the top holdings or a sample that represents a certain percentage of net assets. While the debt multiple varies depending on the fund, the trend in general has followed the same path as the broader market – steadily rising since the Global Financial Crisis, reflecting a supportive backdrop.

HgCapital Trust is a clear standout in terms of the debt levels being applied to companies in the portfolio with a debt-to-EBITDA ratio above that of the market. The ratio for Princess Private Equity is broadly in line with the market but the remaining funds have debt levels that are more conservative than market levels. In addition, these funds are investing in relatively defensive businesses, as we highlighted previously, where earnings are more consistent and robust which should assist in paying down debt.

The funds in the UK listed private equity universe tend not to adopt significant levels of gearing on a fund level due to the amount of leverage that is applied to the underlying companies within the portfolio. Generally, gearing tends to be limited at around 30% for the investment trusts. Currently, none of the funds discussed in this booklet have gearing over 10%.

That said, the funds make commitments to private equity partnerships which can be drawn down at any stage so the funds must keep a certain level of liquid resources on hand to ensure they can meet calls on capital. The commitments tend to be drawn over a three to five-year period once made and are funded through realisations (exits) of existing investments in the portfolio, while cash and undrawn credit facilities provide a buffer to help meet commitments.

During the Global Financial Crisis in 2008, the UK listed private equity sector suffered a huge sell-off as investors fretted that forward commitments made by these funds could not be financed by either the disposal of existing investments as activity in the market was expected to seize or through bank borrowings as banks would not have the resources for lending.

Table 8 provides a breakdown of the financial position for some of the funds in the UK listed private equity space around the time of the Global Financial Crisis. Given that a number of the funds were established post the crisis, we only have data on HgCapital Trust, Aberdeen Private Equity Opportunities, CT Private Equity, ICG Enterprise Trust and Pantheon International. Nonetheless, the table gives a sense of the level of commitments at that time.

Table 8: Summary Balance Sheets during GFC

Fund	Date	NAV	Net Cash / Debt	Undrawn Credit	O/s Commit-ments	Unfunded Commit-ments	% of NAV
		£m	£m	£m	£m	£m	
HgCapital Trust	Dec. 2008	234	130	25	300	145	62.0%
Abrdn PE Opportunities	Sep. 2008	276	28	100	389	261	94.9%
CT Private Equity	Dec. 2008	166	-40	6	158	193	116.3%
ICG Enterprise Trust	Dec. 2008	332	140	0	307	168	50.6%
Pantheon International	Jun. 2008	736	-63	80	641	624	84.8%

Source: Company filings.

Unfunded commitments are any commitments made by funds which are not covered by liquid resources such as cash and undrawn credit facilities. As we can see from the table, these funds had significant amounts of unfunded commitments which were expected to be called upon in the following three to five years – with investors fearing that these funds had overextended themselves during good times.

Ultimately, investors overreacted on the issue of commitments at that time and the funds were able to reduce forward commitments. While investment activity in the market did reduce somewhat, these funds were able to sell down investments to help fund future commitments. In addition, despite the issues in the banking sector, these funds were able to access credit facilities to further assist in meeting commitments.

Table 9 provides an updated breakdown of the financial positions of the funds in the universe. As the table highlights, there is a significant difference in the level of unfunded commitments across the various funds. Of the direct investment funds, APAX Global Alpha, Oakley Capital Investments and HgCapital Trust have relatively high unfunded commitments compared to net asset values. In all three cases, the high level of commitments reflects recent commitments made to in-house funds which are expected to be called over a three to five-year period.

The managers of APAX Global Alpha perform stress test scenarios prior to making commitments to ensure these commitments can be met in more difficult market conditions. In Oakley Capital's case, its existing portfolio is relatively mature, so a significant level of realisations is expected in the short to medium-term which will assist in meeting future commitments.

HgCapital Trust's unfunded commitments are 36.9% of the current NAV. However, the trust is unique in that it invests in its in-house funds at HgCapital (the manager), which have the benefit of opt-out provisions where it can opt out of new investments without penalty should it not have the resources to do so. This is only likely in extreme cases. Nonetheless, it provides the fund with significant flexibility on its commitments.

Table 9: Summary Balance Sheets Today

Fund	Date	NAV	Net Cash / Debt	Undrawn Credit	Outstanding Commit-ments	Unfunded Commit-ments	% of NAV
		£m	£m	£m	£m	£m	
APAX Global Alpha	Sep. 2022	1,402	89	250	1,317	978	69.7%
Dunedin Enterprises	Jun. 2022	75	30	0	10	-20	- 27.2%
HgCapital Trust	Dec. 2022	2,070	294	143	1,200	763	36.9%
NB Private Equity $	Nov. 2022	1,308	5	300	352	47	3.6%
Oakley Capital	Jun. 2022	1,119	97	100	993	796	71.1%
Princess PE €	Oct. 2022	979	27	15	145	103	10.5%
Abrdn PE Opportunities	Nov. 2022	1,123	20	239	708	450	40.0%
CT Private Equity	Jun. 2022	478	-15	95	179	98	20.6%
HarbourVest Global	Jul. 2022	3,815	229	800	2,791	1,762	46.2%
ICG Enterprise Trust	Jul. 2022	1,269	13	161	528	354	27.9%
Pantheon International	Nov. 2022	2,476	52	508	848	288	11.6%

Source: Company filings.

Historically, funds of funds have been managed with slightly higher commitments due to the different timelines at which they expect the underlying funds to call commitments. In addition, it is often the case that a portion of commitments are never called. For example, the manager of ICG Enterprise Trust highlighted that it is typical for funds not to draw down more than 90% of commitments made. Of ICG Enterprise Trust's current £528 million of outstanding commitments, £95 million is to funds outside their investment period so are unlikely to be called in.

HarbourVest Global implements an over-commitment strategy as it aims to remain fully invested over time – which explains the significant £2.8 billion of future commitments. To provide flexibility in more challenging macroeconomic environments, HarbourVest has in place a large credit facility with an extended life. During the Global Financial Crisis in 2008/09, HarbourVest Global performed robustly as a result, being a net investor through the period from 2008 to 2011. ICG Enterprise Trust and Abrdn Private Equity Opportunities adopt similar strategies.

In summary, at an underlying portfolio level, debt multiples are now back at the peak levels seen in 2007 prior to the crisis. However, on average, these companies are high margin, defensive and cash-generative businesses which should be supportive for debt pay down. The funds in the UK listed private equity universe also have lower levels of unfunded commitments today compared to the levels seen during the Global Financial Crisis in 2008 – and, in our view, the funds should not have issues satisfying commitments in the coming years.

Valuation Risk

Similar to financial risk, our analysis of valuation risk can be done at both an underlying portfolio level by examining valuation metrics for the average company in the funds' portfolios along with the broader private equity space as a whole, and at a fund level by looking at discount/premiums to net asset value at which the share prices are trading at in the market and how these compare to historic levels through the cycle.

Valuations have been on the rise in private equity markets since the Global Financial Crisis in 2008 which reflects, in part, the declining interest rate environment highlighted in *Chart 4* earlier.

Chart 7 provides a breakdown of median EV-to-EBITDA[8] ratios, the common valuation metric used in private equity, for the buyout markets in

---

[8] Enterprise Value divided by Earnings before Interest, Tax, Depreciation and Amortisation (EBITDA). The Glossary contains a full explanation.

both Europe and the US compared to global public equity markets as represented by the MSCI World Index. The data on the US private equity market and the MSCI World Index is from 2006 to 2021, while it is from 2010 to 2021 on the European market.

Chart 7: Private Equity Market EV-to-EBITDA Ratio

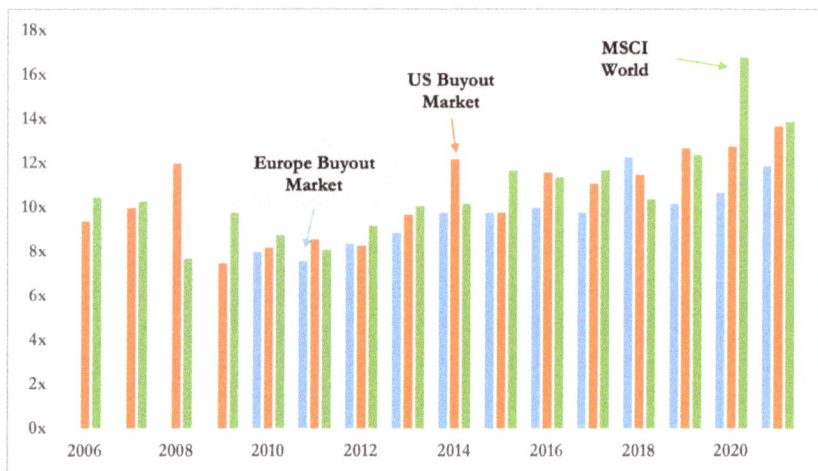

Source: Pitchbook.

Similar to the debt-to-EBITDA multiples for the market, figures differ depending on the provider. For consistency, we have again used data provided by Pitchbook.

At the end of December 2021, the median EV-to-EBITDA ratio for US buyouts was 13.7x while the equivalent ratio for the European market was 11.9x. As the chart highlights, these valuation multiples have been rising since the beginning of the 2010s and, in the case of the US market, have surpassed the previous peak levels prior to the Global Financial Crisis. While we do not have the data back to pre-crisis years, it is likely that the European market has also surpassed the previous peak. In comparison, the EV-to-EBITDA ratio for the MSCI World Index has followed a similar pattern – gradually rising over the last decade or so and surpassing the levels reached just before the crisis in 2008.

Chart 8 provides the average EV-to-EBITDA ratio for each of the funds at the most recent reported date. Similar to debt-to-EBITDA ratios, these funds report the average figure for a sample of the portfolio based on the top holdings or a sample that represents a certain percentage of net assets.

Chart 8: EV-to-EBITDA Ratio by Fund

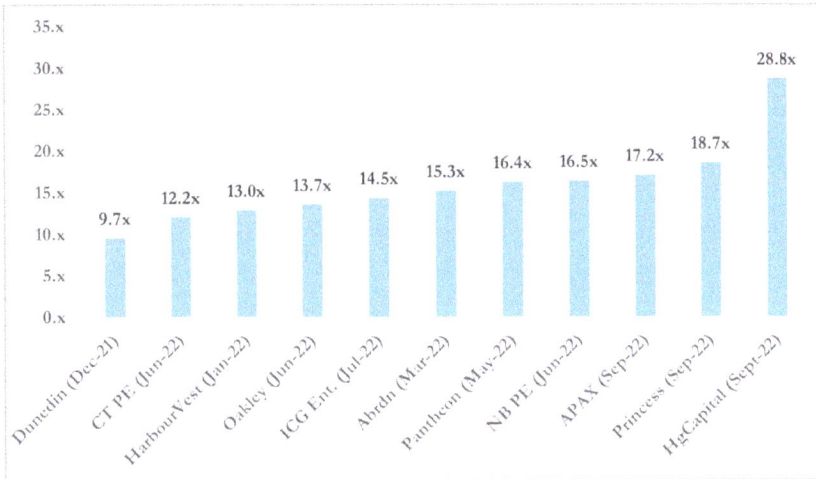

Source: Most recent company filings.

HgCapital Trust is again the clear standout with an average EV-to-EBITDA ratio of 28.8x, well above the market levels, and reflects its focus on technology companies, an area that has been highly prized by investors in recent years. CT Private Equity, Dunedin Enterprises and HarbourVest Global are all trading on average multiples below the broader private equity market.

The remaining funds have average ratios that are above the broader market. However, as *Table 4* highlighted, the underlying companies within the funds' portfolios have been delivering strong growth over the last decade so a premium rating to the market average is warranted.

We outlined the role of declining interest rates over the last decade or so which have been the driver of the rising valuation multiples highlighted in the above charts. With access to 'easy' capital at low interest rates, private equity firms have been willing to pay higher and higher prices for companies – pushing valuation multiples to elevated levels. Since the end of 2021, however, it is likely that we entered a new era of higher interest rates with central banks raising rates around the world. As a result, it is likely that valuations will have to come down from current levels.

A unique feature of the UK listed private equity funds in general is that their shares are priced on a daily basis in the market and can fluctuate from trading on premiums and discounts to net asset values (NAVs). As these funds only report net asset values on a periodic basis, the level of discounts or premiums can reflect investors' expectations of net asset values, so a premium rating (or tighter than average discount) would indicate the expectation of a higher NAV, while a wider than usual discount would indicate that investors are expecting NAV downgrades in the future.

Chart 9: Average Discount to NAV in UK Listed Private Equity Universe (ex 3i Group)

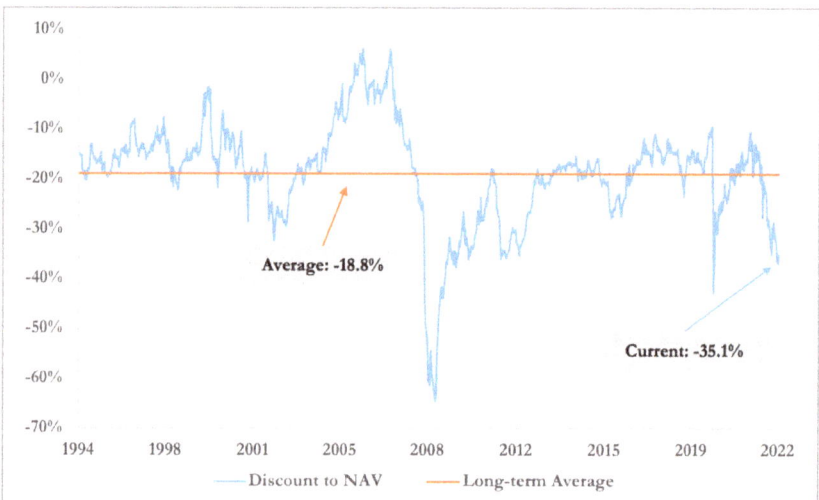

Source: Bloomberg.

Chart 9 highlights the average discount/premium to net asset value for the funds in the UK listed private equity space (ex 3i Group) back to 1994 – with clear fluctuations through time. During times of market stress, discounts have widened significantly.

Prior to the dot-com bubble in the late 1990s, the average discount was close to par (*i.e.* zero) but widened significantly to over 30% in the following three years. Most severe was during the Global Financial Crisis in 2008 which, as we discussed previously, reflected investors' concerns over the funds' ability (or possible inability) to meet large future commitments. Discounts in the space widened once again during the onset of the coronavirus pandemic in 2020.

More recently, we have seen a further sell-off in the share prices of these funds reflecting investors' fears over NAV downgrades (which come with a lag) given (i) rising interest rates (ii) a possible economic slowdown (and potential recession) impacting underlying earnings growth and (iii) valuations placed on individual investments in these funds are likely to decline in line with the declines that have already taken place in the public equity market.

We can further emphasise this widening of discounts in *Table 10* – highlighting each fund's current discount to NAV and its average discount/premium to NAV since inception of each fund. As the table highlights, with the exception of Dunedin Enterprises, current discounts to NAV are all at a wider level than the average discount. And, in some cases, the current discounts are significantly wider than the long-term average.

The current levels are a rare occurrence – with today's discounts only reaching a wider level on two previous occasions since 1994 as highlighted in *Chart 9*. In *Table 10* we also provide a breakdown of the NAV downgrades currently being priced in by investors – based on each fund's average discount since inception.

In the case of ICG Enterprise Trust, Pantheon International and Princess Private Equity, investors are pricing in NAV downgrades that are not far from the write-downs seen during the Global Financial Crisis in 2008.

Investors' concerns are not without reason given the current economic and market environment, and NAV downgrades are a strong possibility going forward – with some modest downgrades already coming through for some of the funds. However, the current discounts to NAVs on offer from the majority of these funds have priced in a lot of the risks and, in our view, are providing a significant margin of safety.

Table 10: Individual Fund Discount to NAV Data

	Inception	Discount to NAV	Average since Inception	NAV Decline Priced In*	NAV Decline during GFC	NAV Decline Dot-com Bubble
APAX Global Alpha	2015	-24.9%	-15.7%	-11.0%	-	-
Dunedin Enterprises	1994	-11.7%	-21.6%	-	-27.2%	-
HgCapital Trust	1994	-22.2%	-11.2%	-12.4%	-20.1%	-23.3%
NB Private Equity	2009	-31.7%	-26.3%	-7.1%	-28.2%	-
Oakley Capital	2007	-36.0%	-23.4%	-16.4%	-	-
Princess PE	2007	-40.1%	-23.4%	-21.9%	-25.0%	-
Abrdn PE Opportunities	2005	-37.7%	-18.3%	-23.7%	-42.2%	-
CT Private Equity	2001	-35.6%	-21.6%	-17.8%	-22.8%	-21.1%
HarbourVest Global	2010	-43.8%	-25.7%	-24.4%	-	-
ICG Enterprise Trust	1994	-32.9%	-18.2%	-17.9%	-21.8%	-25.0%
Pantheon International	1994	-45.7%	-22.0%	-30.4%	-33.0%	-24.8%

* *Based on the average discount since inception.*

Source: Bloomberg.

Private equity offers investors access to managers with a long-term focus who take stakes in private companies and aim to generate returns by improving and growing businesses through a range of measures, including operational improvements, enabling investment for the future, strengthening management teams, and making better use of the balance sheet. Investors are attracted to private equity due to the potential for above average returns on investments with private equity historically delivering higher returns than public equity markets.

Traditional private equity funds are difficult to access for retail investors due to high minimum investment requirements, long-term lock-in periods and high upfront fees. However, the UK listed private equity sector, a sub-sector of the broader private equity market, offers an alternative. It is a universe of liquid investment funds which are listed on the London Stock Exchange and have no minimum size of investment or lock-up periods.

The managers of these funds are investing in private companies and tend to focus on businesses generating strong and consistent cash flows which are operating in markets with growth tailwinds and have strong balance sheets. And, over time, these funds have demonstrated an ability to invest in companies that are delivering strong revenue and profit growth which, in turn, has been the driver of these funds delivering strong NAV growth over the long-term.

Rising valuation multiples have also contributed to NAV growth in recent years with valuations in private equity markets steadily rising over the last decade and are now above the previous cycle peak in 2007. Debt levels have also been rising and the median net debt to EBITDA ratio for both the US and European market are now above 6 and back at levels not seen since the previous peak in 2007.

The market backdrop of low interest rates and easy access to capital has been supportive of asset prices in general since the Global Financial Crisis, and private equity investors have benefited as a result. Looking forward, however, NAV growth for the funds in the space will likely be harder to come by compared to recent years. This reflects a rising interest rate environment, the fact that debt used to fund individual private equity deals are at historically high levels, the possibility of an economic slowdown impacting underlying earnings growth and the current high valuations placed on individual investments in these funds.

That said, share price discounts to net asset values for the funds in the UK listed private equity space have widened significantly over the last year, reflecting these concerns and are pricing in large NAV downgrades. In our view, the discounts account for a significant amount of the risks mentioned above and provide a margin of safety for investors in quality private equity funds.

There are risks for sure in private equity, but dealing with risks is a key part of investing and this is the case for all markets. Private equity is an interesting sub-area of capital markets where access to high quality managers offers the potential of generating higher returns than public equity markets over the long-term. The market is accessible to all with the UK listed private equity space providing an attractive way of gaining exposure to private equity markets, in our view, without the need for significant minimum investments and long-term lock-in period which are prevalent in traditional unlisted private equity funds.

For investors interested in investing in private equity markets, but who may not have the time or capacity to invest through traditional private equity partnerships, the UK listed private equity space provides access to all.

Fund Profiles

We provided a list of 11 funds at the beginning of this booklet which were referenced throughout. In the following pages we profile three of the funds from the UK listed private equity universe: HgCapital Trust, Pantheon International and Princess Private Equity.

4: FUND PROFILE: HgCAPITAL TRUST

HgCapital Trust is a London-listed private equity investment trust managed by HgCapital, a private equity investment house with over £40 billion of assets under management. The trust aims to provide consistent long-term returns to shareholders by investing predominantly in unlisted companies where value can be created through strategic and operational changes. The manager specialises in defensive growth leveraged buyouts in technology and related services businesses.

Share Price (**31 Dec. 2022**)	£3.51
NAV per share	£4.54
Market value	£1.61 billion
Net assets	£2.07 billion
Ticker code	HGT LN
ISIN	GB00BJ0LT190
Fund type	Closed-ended Fund
Dividend yield	2.1%
Discount/premium	-22.8%
TER	1.30%
Net Gearing	6.6%

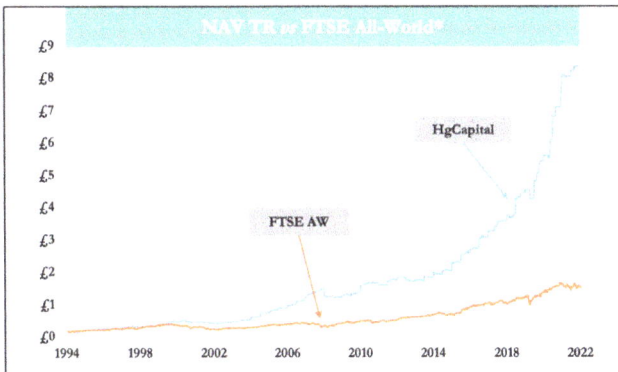

*   *NAV TR = Net Asset Value Total Return; Total Return in Sterling.*
Note: For Personal Retirement Savings Accounts (PRSA) in Ireland, investors may be restricted from trading this security. Please contact your broker for more information.

5: FUND PROFILE: PANTHEON INTERNATIONAL

Pantheon International is a London-listed private equity investment trust managed by Pantheon Ventures, a private equity fund manager with around $88 billion of assets under management. It aims to deliver attractive and consistent returns to investors over the long-term by actively investing in a diversified portfolio of private equity funds and directly in private equity companies. Today, direct investments represent *circa* 44% of the portfolio with the remainder invested in private equity funds.

Share Price (**31 Dec. 2022**)	£2.60
NAV per share	£4.79
Market value	£1.38 billion
Net assets	£2.54 billion
Ticker code	PIN LN
ISIN	GB0004148507
Fund type	Closed-ended Fund
Dividend yield	N/A
Discount/premium	-45.7%
TER	1.15%
Net Gearing	0.0%

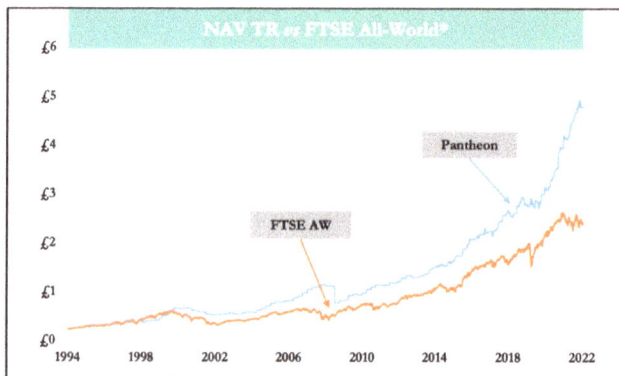

NAV TR *vs* FTSE All-World*

Pantheon

FTSE AW

* Total Return in Sterling.
Note: For Personal Retirement Savings Accounts (PRSA) in Ireland, investors may be restricted from trading this security. Please contact your broker for more information.

6: FUND PROFILE: PRINCESS PRIVATE EQUITY

Princess Private Equity is an investment holding company listed on the London Stock Exchange that invests in a portfolio of private companies. It is managed by Partners Group, a global asset management company with $131 billion under management across private equity, credit, real estate and infrastructure. The fund aims to provide investors with long-term capital growth and an attractive dividend yield by investing in a global portfolio of leading private companies.

Share Price (31-Dec-22)	€8.44
NAV per share	€14.08
Market value	€584 million
Net assets	€974 million
Ticker code	PEY LN
ISIN	GG00B28C2R28
Fund type	Closed-ended Fund
Dividend yield	4.6%
Discount/premium	-40.1%
TER	1.50%
Net Gearing	9.7%

*   Total Return in Sterling.
Note: For Personal Retirement Savings Accounts (PRSA) in Ireland, investors may be restricted from trading this security. Please contact your broker for more information.

APPENDIX

	Management Fee*	Transaction Costs	Performance Fee	Carried Interest
Apax Global Alpha	1.46%	0.04%	0.62%	2.39%
HgCapital Trust	2.00%	0.20%	-	3.10%
NB Private Equity	2.45%	0.19%	-	1.04%
Oakley Capital	2.64%	-	0.53%	4.16%
Princess Private Equity	2.31%	0.10%	2.31%	-
Abrdn PE Opportunities	2.81%	-	-	3.44%
CT Private Equity	1.79%	0.35%	0.88%	-
HarbourVest Global	3.07%	-	-	2.02%
ICG Enterprise Trust	2.75%	0.07%	-	4.12%
Pantheon International	2.37%	0.07%	-	1.56%

* Includes costs such as borrowings, legal fees and other admin costs where applicable.

GLOSSARY

Capital commitments: Capital commitments (or committed capital) is the amount of money limited partners commit to the private equity partnership. These commitments can be called by the general partners at any stage for investment purposes, generally over a three to five-year period. A limited partner who is unable to meet his/her commitment when called upon could face significant penalties based on pre-agreed terms.

EBITDA: EBITDA stands for earnings before interest, tax, depreciation and amortisation and is a widely used measure of core corporate profitability. It attempts to represent cash profits generated by a company by stripping out the non-cash items. However, EBITDA is not a metric recognised under generally accepted accounting principles (GAAP).

Enterprise value (EV): Enterprise value represents the total value of a company defined by its financing. It includes both the value of equity and net debt in the business. Given the significant amount of debt used in private equity investing, enterprise value provides a more accurate value of a company.

EV-to-EBITDA multiple: Enterprise value-to-earnings before interest, tax, depreciation and amortisation. It is the most commonly used valuation metric in private equity.

General partner (GP): In private equity, general partners are the private equity firms which raise capital to launch private equity partnerships. The role of the general partner is to manage the partnership's investments in exchange for fees and a share of the profits above a pre-agreed minimum return rate. Some of the most well-known private equity firms that can be considered general partners include Apollo Global, Blackstone, Carlyle Group and KKR.

Investment holding company: An investment holding company is a company, usually an LLC or corporation, that exists for the sole purpose of holding investments. It does not provide any financial services, nor any other product or service, to the public. These companies are based offshore, usually in the Channel Islands such as Guernsey or Jersey, although they are still listed on the London Stock Exchange.

Investment trust: A closed-end fund which is listed on the stock exchange. The term 'closed-ended' means that there is a fixed number of shares in issue. Once the fund has listed on the stock exchange, any investor who wants to buy into the fund must find another investor in the marketplace who is willing to part with their shares. From the initial share issue, the manager has a fixed amount of capital which is used for investment opportunities with the aim of growing this capital over time. In the UK, under tax rules investment trusts must be registered in the UK meaning investors pay 0.5% stamp duty when buying the shares.

Limited partner (LP): In private equity, a limited partner is a third-party investor in a private equity partnership, providing the capital for the general partnerships to invest on behalf of the limited partners. Examples of limited partners in private equity include public pension funds, corporate pension funds, insurance companies, hedge funds, endowments, foundations, sovereign wealth funds and family offices.

Private equity partnership: A private equity fund which is a closed-end fund not listed on a public stock exchange. The partnership includes both general partners, who are responsible for managing and investing the partnership's assets, and limited partners, the investors who provide the capital for investments.

Private Equity: Access for All

The potential for above average returns has always made private equity an attractive subsector of financial markets with investors gaining access to specialised managers who build portfolios of private companies.

In Ireland, investors' principal way of gaining exposure to private equity has been through international private equity funds distributed by local stockbrokers, which tend to have significant minimum investment amounts and long-term lock-in periods, making access difficult for retail investors.

However, there is an attractive alternative option: investing in high-quality, liquid private equity funds listed on the London Stock Exchange that have historically delivered attractive returns, allowing investors to avoid the high minimum investment levels, long-term lock-in periods and onerous upfront fees.

This booklet, written by Jonathan Yates, research analyst at GillenMarkets, is aimed at providing readers with an overview of private equity investing, including the main characteristics, historical returns, the specifics of the UK listed private equity sector and the key risks investors must be aware of when investing in private equity.

Gillen

E: info@gillenmarkets.com
T: +353 1 2871400
W: www.gillenmarkets.com

www.ingramcontent.com/pod-product-compliance
Lightning Source LLC
Chambersburg PA
CBHW042119190326

41519CB00030B/7550